That's what they said

Published by OH!
20 Mortimer Street
London W1T 3JW

ISBN 978-1-80069-070-7

Compiled by: Sheahan Arnott   Editorial: Theresa Bebbington
Project manager: Russell Porter   Design: Andy Jones
Production: Freencky Portas

A CIP catalogue for this book is available from the Library of Congress

Printed in China

10 9 8 7 6 5 4 3 2

That's what they said

THE LITTLE GUIDE TO
THE OFFICE

CONTENTS

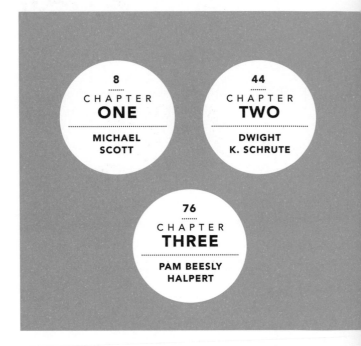

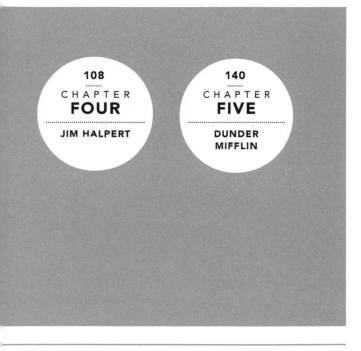

INTRODUCTION

"There is beauty in ordinary things… Isn't that kind of the point?" That's how Pam wrapped up 9 years of a show about a paper company in a city most people have never heard of. And over those 9 seasons there was laughter, cringing, tears, and beauty in the ordinary day-to-day life of Michael, Jim, Dwight, Pam, and the other employees of Dunder Mifflin.

Though it started life as a shot-for-shot remake of the UK version beloved by comedy connoisseurs on both sides of the Atlantic, veteran TV writer and producer Greg Daniels and the creative team on *The Office* soon took the show in its own direction. With Season 1 struggling to find an audience, Michael became more hopeful and less nasty than his UK counterpart David Brent (who has a cameo in Season 7) and the show began to find its footing and flourish.

Now, more than 7 years after Dwight and Angela tied the knot standing in their own graves, *The Office* is the most streamed show in history, and finding new audiences all the time. The show has spawned a new generation of comedies including *Parks and Recreation*, *The Good Place*, and *Brooklyn Nine-Nine* to name but a few. It's given the world podcasts, gifs for every occasion and copycat weddings aboard *The Maid of the Mist*.

And is it that idea of beauty in ordinary things that keeps people coming back? Or do we want to fall in love with Pam and Jim again? Maybe it's because we've all worked with a Michael or a Dwight or a Toby? Because we're confused by Creed, screaming at Kelly to stop getting back with Ryan or revelling in Darryl's climb up the corporate ladder? *The Office* is many things to many people. And isn't that kind of the point?

CHAPTER

ONE

Michael Scott

I want people
to be afraid of how much
they love me.

That's what they said

"

People say I'm the best boss.
They go, 'God, we've never worked
in a place like this. You're hilarious, and
you get the best out of us.'

[lifts up 'World's Best Boss'
coffee mug] Um, I think that pretty
much sums it up. I found it at
Spencer Gifts.

"

*Sometimes if no one will give you the
praise you think you deserve, you have to
give it to yourself. Just look at all the Dundies
Michael won.*

theofficequotes.com – Season 1: Pilot

Michael Scott

66

I guess the attitude that I've tried to create here is that I'm a friend first and a boss second and probably an entertainer third. 99

I think most people who work with him would say that "boss" is a distant third to "friend" and "entertainer" for Michael.

As seen on scarymommy.com, November 21, 2019, by Team Scary Mommy

That's what they said

> **Jim:** Well, I don't think I'll be here in 10 years, but...
>
> **Michael:** That's what I said... That's what she said.
>
> **Jim:** That's what who said?
>
> **Michael:** I never know. But I just say it. I say stuff like that, you know, to lighten the tension when things sort of get hard.
>
> **Jim:** That's what she said.

Jim and Michael reflect on his iconic catchphrase.

As seen on tvfanatic.com – Season 4, Episode 7: Survivor Man

Dunder You Know

Michael says "that's what she said", or a variant of it, 32 times.

It was first used in *Sexual Harassment* (2.02), it's his last line before moving to Denver in *Goodbye, Michael* (7.22), and his first line upon his return in *Finale* (9.26).

The line was said 45 times in total across the show, including by David Brent (Ricky Gervais) during his cameo in *The Seminar* (7.14). The line itself is based on Brent's "said the actress to the bishop" from the original UK version of the show.

66

Would I rather be feared or loved?
Easy. Both. I want people to be afraid
of how much they love me. **99**

*Everything Michael does is in furtherance of his
quest for friendship, love, and acceptance from the
people around him.*

As seen on pastemagazine.com, June 29, 2019,
by Dylan Haas

Michael Scott

66

Toby is in HR which technically means he works for Corporate. So he's not really a part of our family. Also he's divorced... so he's not really a part of his family.

99

Every hero needs a villain.

As seen on brostrick.com, August 1, 2020, by Jennifer Belanger

66

Michael: Ladies and gentlemen. I have some bad news. Meredith was hit by a car.
Jim: What?
Dwight: Where?
Michael: It happened this morning in the parking lot. I took her to the hospital, and the doctors tried to save her life. They did the best that they could... And she is going to be okay.

99

Michael Scott and the art of delivering good news poorly.
As seen on tvfanatic.com – Season 4, Episode 1: Fun Run

Michael Scott

❝

Guess what, I have flaws. What are they? Oh, I don't know. I sing in the shower. Sometimes I spend too much time volunteering. Occasionally I'll hit somebody with my car. So sue me... No, don't sue me. That is the opposite of the point that I'm trying to make.

❞

Everyone has their foibles. Sometimes they might land you in legal hot water.

As seen on theoffice.fandom.com – Dunderpedia: The Office Wiki

66

I enjoy having breakfast in bed. I like waking up to the smell of bacon, sue me. And since I don't have a butler, I do it myself. So, most nights before I go to bed, I will lay six strips of bacon out on my George Foreman Grill. Then I go to sleep. When I wake up, I plug in the grill, I go back to sleep again. Then I wake up to the smell of crackling bacon.

99

When Michael puts it like that, it's a wonder more people don't risk burning their foot on a George Foreman Grill each day.

As seen on goodreads.com

Michael Scott

66

I'm not superstitious, but I am a little 'stitious.

99

After hitting Meredith with his car and Dwight kills Angela's cat, Michael drops an all-time classic when pondering whether the office is cursed.

As seen on studiobinder.com, February 14, 2021, by Kyle Deguzman

---

"

The worst thing about prison was the...
was the Dementors. They... were flying
all over the place, and they were
scary. And they'd come down, and
they'd suck the soul out of your
body, and it hurt!

"

*When Martin starts to compare Dunder Mifflin
unfavorably to prison, only one man can
change everyone's minds… Prison Mike.*

As seen on officequotes.net – Season 3,
Episode 9: The Convict

Dunder You Know

Michael introduces us to 18 of his characters throughout the show. Agent Michael Scarn (a man who it takes more than a bullet to the brain, lungs, heart, back, and balls to kill) appears or is referenced the most – in 6 episodes – while Ping appears 3 times.

His others include Date Mike, Michael Klump, Michael the Magic, and Santa Bond.

That's what they said

66

Yes, it is true. I, Michael Scott, am signing up with an online dating service. Thousands of people have done it, and I am going to do it. I need a username. And I have a great one. Little Kid Lover. That way people will know exactly where my priorities are at.

99

Michael's desire for a family took him to a new frontier. It's safe to assume "Little Kid Lover" was about as successful as Date Mike.

As seen on brostrick.com, August 1, 2020, by Jennifer Belanger

Michael Scott

66

And I knew exactly what to do. But in a much more real sense, I had no idea what to do.

99

Michael is a man for a crisis. Unless that crisis Is Stanley having a heart attack thanks to Dwight's fire drill.

As seen on pastemagazine.com, June 29, 2019, by Dylan Haas

"

An office is not for dying. An office is
a place for living life to the fullest, to
the max, to… an office is a place where
dreams come true.

"

*When your dreams are to be surrounded by
friends and people who love you, then that's
exactly what an office is.*

As seen on cheatsheet.com, January 16, 2019,
by Kamila Rivero

Michael Scott

"

No, Rose, they are not breathing.
And they have no arms or legs…
Where are they? You know what? If we
come across somebody with no arms or
legs do we bother resuscitating them?
I mean, what quality of life do we
have there?

"

*Rose was as ill-prepared for Michael's thoughts
on euthanasia as Michael (and everyone else)
was for CPR training after Stanley's
heart attack.*

As seen on scarymommy.com, October 29, 2019,
by Team Scary Mommy

Dunder You Know

Michael kissing Oscar in *Gay Witch Hunt* (3.01) was completely improvised by Steve Carell – even catching Oscar Nunez off-guard.

The reactions from the cast are authentic, with Jenna Fischer, Mindy Kaling, Angela Kinsey, and Phyllis Smith all struggling not to break character as the camera pans around the room.

Michael Scott

"

There were these huge bins of clothes and everybody was rifling through them like crazy. And I grabbed one and it fit! So, I don't think that this is totally just a woman's suit. At the very least it's bisexual.

"

Between European cut shirts and "bisexual" suits, Michael has a lot of trouble trying to dress to impress.

As seen on theofficequotes.com – Season 3, Episode 18: The Negotiation

---

66

Michael: I DECLARE BANKRUPTCY!
Oscar: I just wanted you to know
that you can't just say the word
'bankruptcy' and expect
anything to happen.
Michael: I didn't say it.
I declared it.

99

*Michael could learn a thing or two about
declaring from Caleb Crawdad.*

As seen on officequotes.net – Season 4,
Episode 4: Money

Michael Scott

66

Michael: Guys! Beef: it's what's
for dinner! Who wants some man
meat?

Dwight: I do! I want some man meat!

Jim: Michael, Dwight would like your
man meat.

Michael: Well then, my man meat
he shall have.

99

*Every great Regional Manager needs a
great Assistant (to the) Regional Manager, and
who could be better than Dwight?*

As seen on tvfanatic.com – Jim Halpert Quotes

66

Jan: I need you to sign these, Michael. It's a waiver of some of your rights. You should read it carefully. It releases the company in the event that our relationship, in your opinion or in reality, interferes with work. You get a copy, I get a copy and a third copy goes to HR.

Michael: Awesome. I'm gonna frame mine. I could frame yours, too.

Jan: You realize this is— This is a legal document that says you can't sue the company—

Michael Scott

Michael: Over our love.

Jan: I've never told you that I love you.

Michael: You don't have to, Jan. This
contract says it all.

99

*Jan and Michael were always doomed to
fail – love contract or no love contract.*

As seen on tvquot.es – Season 3,
Episode 17: Cocktails

66

Michael Scott: Jim, you're 6'11", and you weigh 90 pounds. Gumby has a better body than you. Boom. Roasted. Dwight, you're a kiss-ass. Boom. Roasted. Pam, you failed art school. Boom. Roasted. Meredith, you've slept with so many guys you're starting to look like one. Boom. Roasted. Kevin, I can't decide between a fat joke and a dumb joke. Boom. Roasted. Creed, your teeth called, your breath stinks. Boom. Roasted. Angela, where's Angela? Well, there you are…

I didn't see you behind that grain of rice. Boom. Roasted. Stanley, you crush your wife during sex and your heart sucks. Boom. Roasted. [Stanley starts to laugh] Oscar, you are… Oscar, you're gay.

Oscar: Wow.

Michael Scott: Andy, Cornell called, they think you suck and you're gayer than Oscar. Boom. Roasted. **99**

When Michael's roast doesn't go the way he planned, he returns to the office to exact some revenge. Steve Carell has mentioned since that this tirade would possibly get the show canceled today.

As seen on imdb.com – Season 5, Episode 13: Stress Relief

A Different Dunder Mufflin

More than 30 actors were considered for the role of "Michael Scott" by Greg Daniels and his team, including Dan Aykroyd, Eugene Levy, Stephen Colbert, Ben Falcone, Alan Tudyk, and Martin Short. Rainn Wilson also auditioned for Michael as well as Dwight.

Paul Giamatti was the first person offered the role, and both he and Philip Seymour Hoffman turned it down.

Michael Scott

66

When I said that I wanted to have kids and you said that you wanted me to have a vasectomy, what did I do? And then, when you said that you might want to have kids and I wasn't so sure? Who had the vasectomy reversed? And then when you said you definitely didn't wanna have kids? Who had it reversed back?! Snip snap snip snap snip snap! I did! You have no idea the physical toll that three vasectomies have on a person!

99

Michael and Jan were what happens when unstoppable dysfunction meets the immovable idiot.

As seen on theofficequotes.com – Season 4, Episode 9: Dinner Party

66

Dwight: Michael, what's wrong?

Michael: Everything's wrong. The stress of my modern office has caused me to go into a depression!

Dwight: Depression? Isn't that just a fancy word for feeling bummed out?

Michael: Dwight, you ignorant slut.

99

Michael loves an homage to classic comedy (in this case, Dan Aykroyd) more than he loves making his own jokes.

As seen on tvquot.es – Season 3,
Episode 19: Safety Training

Michael Scott

> I say dance, they say 'How high?'
>
> I'm an early bird and I'm a night owl so I'm wise and I have worms.
>
> You know what they say. Fool me once, strike one, but fool me twice... strike three.

Michael Scott: putting the "idiot" into idioms.

As seen on pastemagazine.com, June 29, 2019, by Dylan Haas

"

I cannot keep myself from Michael. Everything he does is sexy. He has this undeniable animal magnetism. He's a jungle cat. The man exudes sex. He can put both his legs behind his head. **"**

Holly Flax

Yes, it's hard to believe that a man with Michael Scott's sexual energy stayed single for so long.

As seen on tvquot.es – Season 7, Episode 15: PDA

Michael Scott

❝

Don't ever, for any reason, do anything for anyone, for any reason, ever, no matter what. No matter where. Or who, or who you are with, or where you are going or… or where you've been… ever. For any reason, whatsoever. **❞**

When David Wallace invites Michael to New York to see what the rest of the company can learn from Dunder Mifflin Scranton's success, he quickly finds out that Michael may not be the brilliant mind he appears to be.

As seen on scarymommy.com, October 29, 2019, by Team Scary Mommy

---

"

Sometimes I'll start a sentence,
and I don't even know where it's
going. I just hope I find it along the
way. Like an improv conversation.
An improversation.

"

*It's important to keep yourself guessing, but
unfortunately David Wallace doesn't find any
value in Michael's "improversations".*

As seen on officequotes.net – Season 5,
Episode 11: The Duel

66

I love inside jokes. I'd love to be a part of one someday.

99

Michael's sad reflection on a life making others laugh, yet having no one to laugh with. Until Holly.

As seen on comicbookandbeyondy.com, June 5, 2019, by Alex Parale

---

That's what they said

> 66
>
> Society teaches us that having feelings and crying is bad and wrong. Well, that's baloney, because grief isn't wrong. There's such a thing as good grief. Just ask Charlie Brown. 99

After his former boss Ed Truck dies, Michael is forced to confront his own mortality and questions who will mourn him when he dies. Thankfully Pam and a dead bird help him see the people who care about him.

As seen on pastemagazine.com, June 29, 2019,
by Dylan Haas

Michael Scott

66

The people that you work with are just, when you get down to it, your very best friends. They say on your deathbed, you never wish you spent more time at the office, but I will.

99

Michael's last talking head before he leaves Scranton to start his new life with Holly says everything you need to know about him and his love for his co-workers.

As seen on officequotes.net – Season 7, Episode 21: Goodbye Michael

CHAPTER

TWO

Dwight K. Schrute

Determined,
Worker, Intense, Good worker,
Hard worker, Terrific.

66

How would I describe myself?
Three words: hardworking, alpha male,
jackhammer, merciless, insatiable. **99**

*Dwight may be all of those
things – and a great salesman – but counting
to three is beyond him.*

As seen on bayart.org, March 11, 2021, by Deniz Yalim

Dwight K. Schrute

66

Before I do anything, I ask myself,
'Would an idiot do that?'

And if the answer is yes, I do not do
that thing.

99

*A fascinating insight into the mind
of Dwight Schrute.*

*As seen on screenrant.com, September 15, 2020,
by Savannah Di Leo*

> **"**
>
> I come from a long line of fighters. My maternal grandfather was the toughest guy I ever knew. World War II veteran, killed 20 men, and spent the rest of the war in an Allied prison camp. My father battled blood pressure and obesity all his life. Different kind of fight. **"**

When you have generations of Amish beet farmers on one side and German soldiers on the other, you get Dwight.

As seen on pastemagazine.com, February 10, 2013, by Krystle Drew

Dwight K. Schrute

66

I'm gonna live for a very long time.
My grandma Schrute lived to be 101.
My grandpa Manheim is 103, and
still puttering around in Argentina.
I tried to go visit him once, but my
travel visa was protested by the
Shoah Foundation.

99

*Dwight's heritage is peculiar at best, and a
matter for the Nuremberg Trials at worst.*

As seen on tvfanatic.com – Season 4,
Episode 2: Dunder-Mifflin Infinity

That's what they said

66

I did not become a Lackawanna County
volunteer sheriff's deputy to make friends.
And by the way, I haven't.
99

*If you don't make friends, then your
swift and righteous Schrute justice can't be
influenced by them.*

As seen on thequiz.com, January 15, 2019, by Kali Pye

Dwight K. Schrute

"

Would I ever leave this company?
Look, I'm all about loyalty. In fact,
I feel like part of what I'm being paid
for here is my loyalty. But if there were
somewhere else that valued loyalty
more highly... I'm going wherever
they value loyalty the most.

"

You can't put a price on loyalty –
unless you're Dwight.

As seen on pastemagazine.com, February 10, 2013,
by Krystle Drew

66

Dwight: We're third cousins, which is great for bloodlines and isn't technically incest.
Jim: Right in the sweet spot.

99

It's hard to strike the right balance between shrinking the gene pool and keeping it in the family.

As seen on scarymommy.com, September 21, 2020, by Deirdre Kaye

Dwight K. Schrute

"

Congratulations on your one cousin.
I have 70, each one better than
the last.

"

*It's not clear where Mose ranks on the list
but one way or the other it says a lot about the
other 69 Schrute cousins.*

As seen on pastemagazine.com, February 10, 2013,
by Krystle Drew

66

Mose is my cousin and he lives here.
He will always be my best friend.
Unless things go well with Ryan today,
in which case, I won't hang out
with Mose so much anymore. 99

*Dwight's famous loyalty clearly extends
beyond the walls of Dunder Mifflin.*

As seen on officequotes.net – Season 3,
Episode 5: Initiation

Dwight K. Schrute

"
Now that I own the building, I'm looking for new sources of revenue. And a daycare center? Muahahahahahahahaha… Well I guess it's not an evil idea, it's just a regular idea, but there's no good laugh for a regular idea. **"**

It may not be an evil idea, but the daycare center he and Mose set up was the stuff of nightmares.

As seen on bayart.org, March 11, 2021,
by Deniz Yalım

That's what they said

66

I have been Michael's number two guy for about 5 years, and we make a great team. We're like one of those classic famous teams. He's like Mozart and I'm like Mozart's friend. No. I'm like Butch Cassidy and Michael is like Mozart. You try and hurt Mozart, you're gonna get a bullet in the head, courtesy of Butch Cassidy. **99**

Ah yes the classic duo… Butch Cassidy and the Magic Flute Kid. Little known fact - Mozart actually wrote "Raindrops Keep Falling on My Head".

As seen on ponbee.com, February 12, 2020, by Brian Zeng

Dwight K. Schrute

"

I grew up on a farm. I have seen animals having sex in every position imaginable. Goat on chicken. Chicken on goat. Couple of chickens doing a goat, couple of pigs watching.

"

What they don't tell you about farms is that they're a veritable animal orgy at all times.

As seen on tvquot.es – Season 3, Episode 20: Product Recall

That's what they said

66

People say, 'Oh it's dangerous to keep weapons in the home, or the workplace.' Well I say, it's better to be hurt by someone you know, accidentally, than by a stranger, on purpose.

99

Thankfully Dwight had his pepper spray handy when Roy came to the office looking for blood. Even if Roy was someone they knew coming to hurt Jim on purpose.

As seen on theoffice.fandom.com – Dunderpedia:
The Office Wiki

Dwight K. Schrute

66

Security in this office park is a joke.
Last year I came to work with my spud-
gun in a duffel bag. I sat at my desk all
day with a rifle that shoots potatoes at
60 pounds per square inch. Can you
imagine if I was deranged? 99

Yes, just imagine if Dwight was a crazy person.

As seen on pastemagazine.com, February 10, 2013,
by Krystle Drew

66

Jim: 'It is your birthday,' period.
   Not even an exclamation point?
Dwight: It's a statement of fact.
   This is more professional. It's not
   like she discovered a cure
   for cancer.
Jim: I can't believe how bad this looks.

Dwight K. Schrute

Dwight: Are you trying to hurt my feelings? Because if so, you are succeeding.

Fortunately my feelings regenerate at twice the speed of a normal man's.

99

Not everyone can be good at everything.

As seen on imdb.com – Season 5, Episode 14: Lecture Circuit Part 1

66

Dwight: You know, you can always refinance your mortgage. We had a 15-year on our beet farm, we paid it off early.

Michael: Yeah, well, you know what? Nobody cares about your stupid beet farm. Beets are the worst.

Dwight: People love beets.

Michael: Nobody likes beets.

Dwight: Everyone loves beets.

Michael: Nobody likes beets, Dwight. Why don't you grow something that everybody does like? You should grow candy. I'd love a piece of candy right now. Not a beet. ”

Dwight is a beet farmer as a nod to series creator Greg Daniels' grandparents, who farmed beets in Poland.

As seen on imdb.com – Season 2, Episode 3: Office Olympics

66

I wish I could menstruate. If I could menstruate, I wouldn't have to deal with idiotic calendars anymore. I'd just be able to count down from my previous cycle. Plus I'd be more in tune with the moon and the tides.

99

Menstruation is all upside according to Dwight.

As seen on pastemagazine.com, February 10, 2013, by Krystle Drew

Dwight K. Schrute

"

I saw *Wedding Crashers* accidentally.
I bought a ticket for *Grizzly Man* and
went into the wrong theater. After
an hour, I figured I was in the wrong
theater, but I kept waiting. Cuz that's
the thing about bear attacks... they
come when you least expect it. **"**

If only he'd stayed until the post-credits scene
where Vince Vaughn is mauled by a bear.

As seen on dailycal.org, January 30, 2020,
by Zachary Abduel-Saud

That's what they said

"

Women are like wolves. If you
want one you must trap it. Snare it.
Tame it. Feed it. **"**

*Angela may prefer to be compared to a cat,
rather than a wolf.*

As seen on bighivemind.com, February 28, 2018

Dwight K. Schrute

66

I don't have a lot of experience with vampires, but I have hunted werewolves. I shot one once, but by the time I got to it, it had turned back into my neighbor's dog.

99

Hate it when that happens.

❝

Dwight: Yee-haw! Woo-hoo! [Dwight imitates a gun firing in the air] Howdy, partners. It's me, Gun Safety Dwight. And I'm the rootin'-est… I can't do this. Um, look, obviously a gun went off under my watch and I'm launching a full investigation.
Stanley: We all saw you do it. **❞**

Dwight channels his inner Michael after someone (he) fires a gun in the office.

As seen on bighivemind.com, February 28, 2018

Dwight K. Schrute

66

Dwight: It's gonna be okay.

Angela: How's it gonna be okay, Dwight? Everyone will know our business.

Dwight: Well, that's not the worst thing in the world. I'll just stand up in front of the office and reveal our true love. It won't be that bad. Look at Kelly and Ryan.

Angela: I hate those two people more than anything in the entire world. **99**

Ryan and Kelly are not the #relationshipgoals you want to measure yourself against.

As seen on tvquot.es – Season 3, Episode 12: Traveling Salesmen

That's what they said

> **"** Listen to me! I love you! And I don't care that Phillip's not my son! I will raise 100 children with 100 of your lovers if it means I can be with you! **"**

Jim and Pam's journey pales in comparison to Dwight and Angela, who had to survive dead cats, multiple engagements, farm machinery agreements and Staples to be together as man and wife.

As seen on ponbee.com, February 12, 2020, by Brian Zeng

Dwight K. Schrute

66

Why tip someone for a job I'm capable of doing myself? I can deliver food. I can drive a taxi. I can, and do, cut my own hair. I did, however, tip my urologist, because I am unable to pulverize my own kidney stones.

99

A man has to have a tipping code – even if it's unfair on the people who have to put up with Dwight.

As seen on whatculture.com, August 21, 2015,
by Sara Weir

That's what they said

"
Jim is my enemy, but it turns out
that Jim is also his own worst enemy.
And the enemy of my enemy is my friend,
so Jim is actually my friend. "

Hard to find fault in Dwight's logic there.

As seen on buzzfeed.com, September 22, 2015, by Andy Golder

Dwight K. Schrute

66

The Shrutes have a word for when everything comes together in a man's life perfectly: Perfectenschlag. Hmm. Right now, I am in it. I finally get a chance to prove myself to Corporate, I am assembling a competent team, I am likely a father, I am so deep inside of perfectenschlag right now. And just to be clear, there is a second definition, 'perfect pork anus', which I don't mean. **99**

But sadly Dwight's special project in Tallahassee goes from one meaning of "perfectenschlag" to another very quickly.

As seen on tvquot.es – Season 8, Episode 14: Special Project

66

Do I get along with my co-workers? Well, first of all, I don't have co-workers anymore, I have subordinates. So... have I gotten along with my subordinates? Let's see. My supplier relations rep, Meredith Palmer, is the only person I know who knows how to properly head bang to Motorhead. Oscar Martinez, my accountant, is now godfather to my son. Angela Schrute, my former accountant, is now my wife.

Dwight K. Schrute

My top salesman, Jim Halpert, was best man at my wedding, and office administrator Pamela Beesly Halpert is my best friend. So…yes. I'd say I have gotten along with my subordinates.

"

Dwight's last line of the series shows just how much he's grown over 9 seasons.

As seen on officequotes.net,
Season 9, Episode 23: Finale

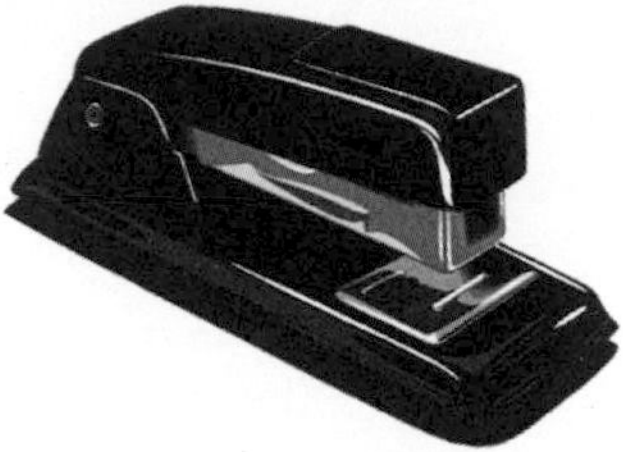

CHAPTER

THREE

Pam Beesly Halpert

There's a lot of beauty in ordinary things. Isn't that kind of the point?

❝

I didn't watch the whole documentary. After a few episodes, it was too painful. I kept wanting to scream at Pam. It took me so long to do so many important things. It's just hard to accept that I spent so many years being less happy than I could have been. Jim was 5 feet from my desk and it took me 4 years to get to him.

It'd be great if people saw this documentary and learned from my mistakes. Not that I'm a tragic person. I'm really happy now. But it would just...

Pam Beesly Halpert

---

just make my heart soar if someone out there saw this and she said to herself 'Be strong, trust yourself, love yourself. Conquer your fears. Just go after what you want and act fast, because life just isn't that long.' **99**

Pam was always the heart of The Office, *and her journey of personal growth and self-discovery was the show's golden thread throughout all 9 seasons.*

As seen on tvquot.es – Season 9, Episode 23: Finale

That's what they said

66

I hate the idea that someone out there hates me. I even hate thinking that al-Qaeda hates me. I think if they got to know me, they wouldn't hate me.

99

SEAL Team 6 were unable to confirm whether or not Osama bin Laden had a box set of The Office *in his compound.*

As seen on sporcle.com, April 25, 2020

Pam Beesly Halpert

66

It's a blessing in disguise. Actually, not even in disguise. Sometimes at home, I answer the phone, 'Dunder-Mifflin, this is Pam.' So, maybe that'll stop now.

99

Pam sees the bright side of the Scranton branch potentially closing.

As seen on officetally.com – Season 3,
Episode 7: Branch Closing

> **"**
> You know what they say about a car wreck, where it's so awful you can't look away? The Dundies are like a car wreck that you want to look away from but you have to stare at it because your boss is making you. **"**

Yes Pam and Roy had a big fight, and yes Pam got so drunk she fell off a chair, but The Dundies (2.01) was the first time she'd kissed Jim and she won the award for "Whitest Sneakers", so maybe it wasn't all bad? Even if she did get banned from Chili's.

As seen on quotegeek.net, April 9, 2013

Pam Beesly Halpert

66

Jim: Hey Pam... I think that's empty.
Pam: No, 'cause the ice melts and then
it's like... second drink! **99**

*There's not a person in the world who has
finished the icy remains of a cocktail and not
thought about "second drink".*

As seen on theofficequotes.com – Season 2,
Episode 1: The Dundies

> **"**
> Roy and I just got back from the Poconos. I get 10 vacation days a year, and I try to hold off taking them for as long as possible, and this year I got to the third week in January. **"**

Pam is definitely the type to eat her lunch at 11am because she's too hungry to wait.

As seen on needsomefun.net, June 28, 2020,
by Ugur Oral

Pam Beesly Halpert

" I don't often miss Roy, but I can tell you one thing. I wish someone had flashed me when I was with Roy. Because that would have been the ass-kicking of the year. Especially if it had been Jim. He would not have wanted me to have seen Jim's— Whoo, I'm… I am saying a lot of things. **"**

Given how Roy reacted when Pam told him Jim had kissed her, Roy might have left Jim a eunuch (if Dwight wasn't there to defend him).

As seen on tvquot.es – Season 3, Episode 21:
Women's Appreciation

66

I've decided that I'm going to be more honest. I'm gonna start telling people what I want directly. So look out world 'cause old Pammy is getting what she wants. And don't call me Pammy.

99

Roy was the only character to call her "Pammy" and this was symbolic of Pam's growth as a person away from him and their relationship.

As seen on officetally.com – Season 3, Episode 17: Cocktails

Pam Beesly Halpert

> **"** There's nothing better than a beautiful day at the beach, filled with sun, surf, and… uh, diligent note-taking. **"**

Dunder Mifflin's annual Beach Day starts with Michael tasking Pam with helping him find his replacement, and ends with her telling everyone – especially Jim – what she thinks of them.

As seen on screenrant.com, March 28, 2019,
by Amanda Steele

"

Jim, I called off my wedding because of you. And now we're not even friends. And things are just, like, weird between us, and that sucks. And I miss you. You were my best friend before you went to Stamford. And I really miss you. I shouldn't have been with Roy. And there were a lot of reasons to call off my wedding. But the truth is, I didn't care about any of those reasons until I met you. And now you're with someone else. And that's fine. It's... Whatever.

Pam Beesly Halpert

That's not what I'm... I'm not... Okay,
my feet really hurt. The thing that
I'm just trying to say to you, Jim, and to
everyone else in the circle, I guess,
is that I miss having fun with you.
Just you, not everyone in the circle.
Okay, I am gonna go walk in the
water now. **99**

Pam's iconic Beach Day speech.

As seen on imdb.com – Season 3,
Episode 22: Beach Games

> **"** Every time Michael's in a meeting, he makes me come in and give him a Post-it note telling him who's on the phone. I did it once, and he freaked out. He loved it so much. The thing is, he doesn't get that many calls. So he has me make them up every 10 minutes. **"**

You miss 100% of the fake calls you don't take.

As seen on tvquot.es – Season 4,
Episode 8: The Deposition

Pam Beesly Halpert

66

Oh God no, Dwight isn't my friend…
Oh my God! Dwight's kind of
my friend!

99

*Dwight's concussion is the start of a beautiful
friendship.*

As seen on needsomefun.net, June 28, 2020,
by Ugur Oral

That's what they said

> Dunder Mifflin. This is Pam. Hi, David. No, I'm sorry. He's not back from the civil rights rally. I'll have him call you the minute he gets back from the Lincoln Memorial. [To camera] When Michael's skirting a phone call, he gave me a list of places to say he is. 'Stopping a fight in the parking lot.' 'An Obama fashion show.' Whatever that is. Or 'Trapped in an oil painting.' I'm gonna save that one.

If Pam did tell the truth about where Michael was, it might sound as ridiculous as his made-up ones.

As seen on tvfanatic.com – Season 5,
Episode 19: Golden Ticket

Pam Beesly Halpert

66

Dwight: Well something's come up,
  I have to go.
Pam: No no no no no! She'll wake up!
Dwight: I have something to do.
Pam: Look, I know what you have to do,
  please stay with Cece. Dwight? I've always
  considered for us to be very good friends.
  Great friends! Remember your concussion?
Dwight: I do. But you married my
  worst enemy.

99

*When Dwight is the only person who can
stop Cece from crying, Pam does everything
she can to make sure he can stay with them
and not hook-up with Angela.*

As seen on officequotes.net – Season 7,
Episode 8: Viewing Party

"

Jan: You know, the company is
offering a design training program in
New York.

Pam: Well, I have a job right now. So,
I can't really take time off.

Jan: Well, it's only on weekends. And
then a few weeks in New York, but
I'm sure that I could ask Corporate to
help you out.

Pam Beesly Halpert

Pam: Well, it's just that the weekends aren't good because—
Jan: There are always a million reasons not to do something. **99**

Before her descent into madness,
Jan was all in on supporting Pam's art – even
dropping one of the show's best pearls of
real-life wisdom.

As seen on officetally.com – Season 2,
Episode 15: Boys and Girls

That's what they said

66

Pam: I was hoping for a righteous mob, and I ended up with Dwight and Nellie. But, they both have a mob mentality. And, I'm pretty sure Dwight has a pitchfork in his car.
Dwight: You need my pitchfork?

99

Frank defacing Pam's mural is the start of everyone's least favourite storyline – Pam & Boom Mic Brian. At least Brian was there to stop Frank from assaulting Pam.

As seen on tvquot.es – Season 9, Episode 14: Vandalism

Pam Beesly Halpert

"

Jan used to be one of my superiors, and she is one of the most erratic and terrifying people I have ever met. Jim and I are pretty sure she had an affair with her ex-assistant Hunter. He was 17. But she looks great. If she asks, will you tell her I said that? **"**

After she's fired from Dunder Mifflin and shacks up with Michael, Pam and Michael's history is enough for Jan to dislike Pam.

As seen on officequotes.net – Season 9, Episode 7: The Whale

"

Dwight mercy-killed Angela's cat. It's very complicated. It's caused a lot of unpleasantness between Dwight and Angela. Who were both already prone to unpleasantness.

"

The death of Sprinkles was also the death of Dwight and Angela – much to Pam's chagrin.

As seen on officequotes.net – Season 4, Episode 3: Launch Party

---

Pam Beesly Halpert

66

I am actually looking forward to
'Take Your Daughter to Work Day.'
I am not great with kids, but I wanna
get better because I'm getting married.
So I put out a bunch of extra candy
on my desk so the kids will come
talk to me. Like the witch in Hansel
and Gretel.

99

*The only "daughter" Pam ends up bonding
with is Meredith's son, Jake. Maybe he
remembered shredding paper with her
when he showed up as the entertainment for
Angela's bachelorette party?*

As seen on theoffice.fandom.com – Dunderpedia:
The Office Wiki

66

Michael: You and Jim are close, huh?
Pam: Yeah, I think the pregnancy really
brought us together.

99

*Funny how having a baby with someone will
do that.*

As seen on ew.com – Season 6,
Episode 2: The Meeting

Pam Beesly Halpert

66

I used to love coming here. The chicken parm is good. Big part of my childhood. Oh, maybe Michael will start dating that too.

99

Pam did not embrace Michael as a potential new step-dad.

As seen on quizlet.com – Season 6,
Episode 8: Double Date

That's what they said

"

Jim: Do you remember what you said to me on my first day at work, just before you walked me over to my desk?

Pam: Yeah. 'Enjoy this moment, because you're never going to go back to this time before you met your desk-mate Dwight.'

Jim: And that's when I knew. You?

Pam: You came up to my desk and you said, 'This might sound weird, and there's no reason for me to know this, but that mixed berry yogurt you're about to eat has expired.'

Pam Beesly Halpert

Jim: That was the moment that you knew you liked me?

Pam: Yep.

Jim: Wow. Can we make it a different moment?

Pam: Nope.

99

Not everyone gets to choose their "how we mot" story. Thankfully for Jim and Pam, the rest of their story is far more aww-inspiring.

As seen on tvquot.es – Season 4,
Episode 3: Launch Party

"

Pam: I haven't heard anything. But I bet Jim got the job. I mean, why wouldn't he? He's totally qualified and smart. Everyone loves him. And if he never comes back again, that's okay. We're friends. And I'm sure we'll stay friends. We just—

We never got the timing right. You know, I shot him down and then he did the same to me and— But you know what, it's okay. I'm totally fine. Everything is going to be totally—

Pam Beesly Halpert

Jim: Pam. Sorry. Are you free for dinner
  tonight?
Pam: Yes.
Jim: All right. Then it's a date.
Pam: [To camera] I'm sorry. What was
  the question?

*The moment we waited so long for
was everything it needed to be and more.*

As seen on tvquot.es – Season 3, Episode 23: The Job

66

I'm at a crucial point where I have sunk 4 hours into that copier, and I am not going to let it beat me like that wireless router did.

99

Pam's struggles with technology are constant and relatable.

As seen on needsomefun.net, June 28, 2020, by Ugur Oral

Pam Beesly Halpert

> **"** I thought it was weird when you picked us to make a documentary. But all in all, I think an ordinary paper company like Dunder Mifflin was a great subject for a documentary. There's a lot of beauty in ordinary things. Isn't that kind of the point? **"**

Through 9 seasons of laughter and tears, Pam had the honour of delivering the show's last line. And isn't THAT kind of the point?

As seen on upbeacon.com, March 14, 2021,
by Havi Stewart

CHAPTER

FOUR

Jim Halpert

Everything I have I owo to this job.

66

My job is to speak to clients, um, on the phone, about... uh, quantities and, uh, type of... copier paper. You know, whether we can supply it to them, whether they can, uh... pay for it. And, um... I'm... I'm boring myself just talking about this.

99

Only Stanley could lay claim to hating his job more than Jim.

As seen on scatteredquotes.com –
Season 1, Pilot

Jim Halpert

"

Right now, this is just a job. If I advance any higher in this company, this would be my career. And, uh, if this were my career, I'd have to throw myself in front of a train.

"

But Jim did advance – and thankfully there were no nearby trains.

As seen on scarymommy.com, September 21, 2020, by Deirdre Kaye

Dunder You Know?

Most characters do their talking head interviews with the office bull-pen in the background, but Michael does most of his from his office (as do all the characters who have their own office), while Jim usually has an outside-facing window behind him.

The Office's Director of Photography Randall Einhorn came up with shooting characters facing out of the office to show they have a future outside Dunder Mifflin or some internal optimism, while characters who didn't were shot with the office behind them.

Jim Halpert

66

I mean I've always subscribed to the idea that if you really want to impress your boss, you go in there and you do mediocre work, half-heartedly. **99**

And Michael was impressed   Charles Minor less so.

As seen on sporcle.com, April 6, 2020

“

I'm just hiding out until all this stuff blows over. With Creed. Playing chess. At work. He's winning. I feel like I'm describing a dream I had.

”

Almost everything involving Creed sounds like a dream.

As seen on tvfanatic.com – Season 5, Episode 24: Casual Friday

Jim Halpert

66

Jim: I don't know what you want me to tell you, man. All I know is that every time I've been faced with a tough decision, there's only one thing that outweighs every other concern. One thing that will make you give up on everything you thought you knew, every instinct, every rational calculation.

Dwight: Some sort of virus?

Jim: Love.

99

And Jim was there to push Dwight towards Angela again.

As seen on imdb.com – Season 9, Episode 22: A.A.R.M

66

I am about to do something very
bold in this job that I've never done
before: try.

99

*When Ryan starts to put the squeeze on him,
Jim is forced to take drastic measures.*

As seen on womansday.com, February 11, 2020,
by Martha Sorren

Jim Halpert

❝

My roommate wants to meet everybody. Because I'm pretty sure he thinks I'm making Dwight up.

He is very real.

❞

Some people are just so strange that they need to be seen to be believed.

As seen on readbeach.com – Season 2, Episode 9: E-mail Surveillance

66

I miss Dwight.

Congratulations, universe.
You win.

99

When Dwight quits to protect Angela,
Jim is left with Andy and his acapella antics.

As seen on imdb.com – Season 3,
Episode 12: Traveling Salesmen

Dunder You Know?

Jim pranks Dwight 100 times over the course of the show (including deleted scenes), starting with the infamous "stapler in Jell-o" In *Pilot* (1.01) and finishing with "best prank ever" in *Finale* (9.23).

> **Jim:** [Dressed as Dwight] Question, what kind of bear is best?
>
> **Dwight:** That's a ridiculous question.
>
> **Jim:** False. Black bear.
>
> **Dwight:** Well, that's debatable. There are basically two schools of thought.
>
> **Jim:** Fact, bears eat beets. Bears, beets, Battlestar Galactica.
>
> **Dwight:** Bears do not— What is going on? What are you doing?
>
> **Jim:** [To camera] Last week, I was in a drug store and I saw these glasses.

Four dollars. And it only cost me $7 to recreate the rest of the ensemble and that's a grand total of $11.

Dwight: You know what? Imitation is the most sincere form of flattery. So I thank you. [Jim puts a bobblehead on his desk] Identity theft is not a joke, Jim! Millions of families suffer every year! 🙶

Jim's impression of Dwight gave rise to every bad impression of Dwight.

As seen on officequotes.net – Season 3, Episode 20: Product

66

He has not stopped working… for a second. At 12:45, he sneezed while keeping his eyes open, which I always thought was impossible. At 1:32, he peed. And I know that because he did that in an open soda bottle, under the desk, while filling out expense reports. And on the flip side, I've been so busy watching him that I haven't even started work. It's exhausting, being this vigilant. I'll probably have to go home early today.

99

When you hate selling paper so much, why not treat pranking Dwight as a full-time job?

As seen on scarymommy.com, September 21, 2020, by Deirdre Kaye

Jim Halpert

"

I guess, all things considered, I was lucky Dwight was there. And Roy was lucky that Dwight only used pepper spray, and not the nunchucks or the throwing stars. **"**

But despite all the pranks, Dwight was there to protect Jim when he needed it.

As seen on theoffice.fandom.com – Dunderpedia: The Office Wiki

---

Dunder You Know?

John Krasinski and his friends shot some of the footage from the opening credits, including the "Scranton Welcomes You" sign and the Penn Paper and Supply building.

“

Jan is about to have a baby with a sperm donor. And Michael is preparing for the birth of a watermelon with Dwight. Now, this baby will be related to Michael through... delusion. **”**

No one could unpick the ridiculousness of Michael and Dwight – and sometimes Andy – quite like Jim.

As seen on officequotes.net – Season 5,
Episode 3: Baby Shower

66

Jim: Yesterday, we had a meeting about planets.

Michael: Mmm. Well to be fair, Jim... James. Jimothy? [Jim nods] To be fair, Jimothy, ah that sounds weird. Are you okay with being called Jim?

Jim: I am.

Michael: Alright. Jim, to be fair, the conversation wasn't about planets. At first we were talking about introducing a line of toilet paper. And what part of the human body does one use toilet paper upon?

Jim Halpert

Michael: So you draw a line from there to the other planets... and I think by the end we learned a little bit about how small we are. 🙙

When Jim and Michael become co-managers, they struggle to find their rhythm in their new relationship dynamic.

As seen on theofficequotes.com – Season 6, Episode 3; The Promotion

66

Michael: Why am I so sad? Am I doing the wrong thing?

Jim: Absolutely not. It's just that sometimes... goodbyes are a bitch.

Michael: [pulls out a tape recorder and speaks into it] T-shirt idea: 'Goodbyes Stink.' [puts tape recorder away] Okay, alright. So, James Halpert. You started with this company as a fine young man...

Jim: You know what I think we should do? I think we should just save the goodbyes for tomorrow. At lunch.

Michael: Oh, okay.

Jim: And then tomorrow, I can tell you… what a great boss you turned out to be. The best boss I ever had.

99

This was the last scene Steve Carell shot as Michael (before his return in season 9), and it took him and John Krasinski 17 takes to get through it without crying.

As seen on theoffice.fandom.com – Dunderpedia: The Office Wiki

"

Four years ago, I was just a guy who had a crush on a girl who had a boyfriend. And I had to do the hardest thing I've ever had to do, which was just to wait...

...For a really long time, that's all I had. I just had little moments with a girl who saw me as a friend. And a lot of people told me I was crazy to wait this long for a date with a girl who I worked with, but I think even then I knew that I was waiting for my wife.

"

And the wait was worth it for them, and for us.

As seen on goodreads.com

Jim Halpert

66

I ate a tuna sandwich on my first day, so then Andy started calling me 'Big Tuna.' I don't think any of them know my real name.

99

Jim joins "Broccoli Rob" in the pantheon of Andy Bernard food-based nicknames.

As seen on scarymommy.com, September 21, 2020, by Deirdre Kaye

---

That's what they said

66

I bought those tickets the day I saw that YouTube video. I knew we'd need a backup plan. The boat was actually Plan C, the church was Plan B, and Plan A was marrying her a long, long time ago. Pretty much the day I met her. **99**

And after not wanting to marry Roy on a boat during Booze Cruise *(2.11)*, The Maid of the Mist *was the perfect location for Pam to get married.*

As seen on officequotes.net – Season 6,
Episode 4: Niagara

Jim Halpert

❝

I gotta tell you this baby is amazing...
She... gets me out of everything...
And I... and I love her. I also love her
very much.

❞

*Jim took to fatherhood like a duck to water.
Even though Cece couldn't get him out of
spending an evening with Date Mike.*

As seen on officetally.com – Season 6,
Episode 19: Happy Hour

"

If I can make mushed carrots seem better than a boob, I can pretty much sell anything. **"**

Jim Halpert – master salesman

As seen on tvfanatic.com – Season 7,
Episode 9: WUPHF.com

Jim Halpert

66

Jim: Yeah... she's really funny. She's warm... and she's just... yeah.

Michael: Well, if you like her so much, don't give up.

Jim: She's engaged.

Michael: Pfft. BFD. Engaged ain't married.

Jim: Huh.

Michael: Never, ever, ever give up.

99

And Jim took Michael's advice to heart.

As seen on theofficequotes.com – Season 2, Episode 11: Booze Cruise

66

So this year, for the first time ever, I got Pam in Secret Santa. And I got her this teapot, which I know she really wants, so she can make tea at her desk. But I'm also going to stuff it with some inside jokes. Like, this is my high school yearbook photo. She saw it at the party, and it really makes her laugh. Not sure why. What else .. ooh. This is a hot sauce packet. She put this on a hot dog a couple years ago because she thought it was ketchup. And it was

Jim Halpert

really funny, so I kept the other two. [holds up a miniature pencil] This would take a little too long to explain, so I won't. And this is the card. Because Christmas is the time to tell people how you feel. **99**

The famous green teapot was Jim's first big swing at trying to be with Pam.
And it probably inspired a lot of cases for HR departments around the world.

As seen on dundermifflindailyinterview.tumblr.com –
Season 2, Episode 10: Christmas Party

"

Jim: You watched it?
Pam: Yeah.
Jim: Well, then I guess you're ready
  for this.
Pam: What's that?
Jim: It's from the teapot. Everything
  you'll ever need to know is in that
  note. Not enough for me?
  You are everything.

"

*Jim's note was actually a letter from John
Krasinski to Jenna Fischer telling her what their
time together as Jim and Pam meant to him.*

As seen on officequotes.net – Season 9,
Episode 22: A.A.R.M

Jim Halpert

66

Everything I have I owe to this job.
This stupid, wonderful, boring,
amazing job.

99

*The office really was a palace where dreams
came true for Jim.*

As seen on readbeach.com – Season 9,
Episode 23: Finale

CHAPTER

FIVE

Dunder Mifflin

The people person's
paper people.

66

Do I have a special someone?
Well, yeah of course. A bunch of 'em.
My employees.

99

Michael Scott

*You can never dispute that Michael
loved his employees – even if they didn't
always love him.*

As seen on goalcast.com, August 17, 2018,
by Flavia Medrut

❝

Dwight: What about that meeting later to discuss finances?

Angela: Yes. But don't expect any cookie.

Dwight: But what if I'm hungry?

Angela: No cookie.

❞

Dwight and Angela weren't as good at speaking in code as they thought they were…

As seen on imdb.com – Season 2,
Episode 19: Michael's Birthday

That's what they said

66

Kelly: Well I manage my department, and I've been doing that for several years now, and God I've learned a lot of life lessons along the way.
Jim: Your department's just you right?
Kelly: Yes Jim, but I am not easy to manage. **99**

Kelly displays some surprising self-awareness during her interview for Regional Manager.

As seen on tvgag. com – Season 7,
Episode 24: Search Committee

> **"** Ultimatums are key. Basically, nobody does anything for me anymore unless I threaten to kill myself. **"**

Kelly Kapoor,
a woman who knows how to get things done.

As seen on parade.com, March 11, 2020,
by Alexandra Hutado

66

I never really thought about death until Princess Diana died. That was the saddest funeral ever – that, and my sister's.

99

Kelly Kapoor

We all cope with grief differently, but it always hits home more when it's a beloved member of the royal family.

As seen on scarymommy.com, December 21, 2020, by Karen Belz

"

You guys I'm, like, really smart now.
You don't even know. You could ask me,
'Kelly, what's the biggest company in
the world?' And I'd be like, 'blah
blah blah, blah blah blah blah blah
blah.' Giving you the exact
right answer.

"

Kelly Kapoor

*Kelly comes back from Sabre's management
course a new woman – even rebranding as
"Kelly Kapoor – The Business Bitch".*

As seen on scarymommy.com, October 29, 2019,
by Team Scary Mommy

66

I've been involved in a number of cults, both a leader and a follower. You have more fun as a follower, but you make more money as a leader. 99

Creed Bratton

It's not a stretch to picture Creed as one of the Manson Family.

As seen on villains.fandom.com – Season 4, Episode 1: Fun Run

“

Nobody steals from Creed Bratton and gets away with it. The last person to do this disappeared. His name? Creed Bratton.

”

Creed Bratton

Creed is a walking riddle, wrapped in a mystery, inside an enigma.

As seen on imdb.com - Season 5, Episode 4: Crime Aid

❝

Creed Bratton has never declared bankruptcy. When Creed Bratton gets in trouble, he transfers his debt to William Charles Scheider. **❞**

Creed Bratton

"William Charles Scheider" is (the actor) Creed Bratton's real birth name.

As seen on screenrant.com – Season 4, Episode 4: Money

66

I'm not offended by homosexuality.
In the '60s I made love to many, many
women, often outdoors, in the mud
and the rain... and it's possible a man
slipped in. There'd be no way
of knowing.

99

Creed Bratton

When he's not doing "quabbity ashowitz",
Creed is the human Woodstock.

As seen on reddit.com – Season 3,
Episode 1: Gay Witch Hunt

66

We have a gym at home. It's called the bedroom.

As a person who buys a lot of erotic cakes, it's nice to be represented on one.

99

Phyllis Lapin

By the sounds of their relationship, it's lucky Phyllis and Bob Vance (Vance Refrigeration) made it into work most days.

As seen on scarymommy.com, October 29, 2019, by Team Scary Mommy

❝

Well, this is what happened.
Uh, Ryan's big project was the website.
Which wasn't doing so well. So Ryan,
to give the impression of sales,
recorded them twice. Once as offices
and once in the website sales, which
is what we refer to in the business as
misleading the shareholders. Another
good term is fraud. The real crime,
I think, was the beard.

❞

Oscar Martinez

*Oscar sums up Ryan's fall from grace. And his
fall from face.*

As seen on theoffice.fandom.com – Dunderpedia:
The Office Wiki

Dunder You Know?

Phyllis Smith was working as a casting associate for *The Office* when she was offered a part on the show. Greg Daniels was so impressed with how she was reading lines with the auditioning actors that he created the role of Phyllis Lapin (later Vance) specifically for her.

Prior to becoming a casting agent and eventually a desk at Dunder Mifflin, Smith was a professional dancer, burlesque performer and even a cheerleader for the Arizona (then St. Louis) Cardinals in the 1970s!

66

Phyllis: It is so nice to go out with another couple.

Pam: Anything to get out of that office.

Phyllis: I know.

Bob: I honestly don't know how you can work with that jackass, that other jackass, and that new jackass.

Phyllis: He's talking about Michael, Dwight, and Andy.

Jim: Yeah, I understood.

99

Bob Vance (Vance Refrigeration) doesn't hold his Scranton Office Park neighbors in high regard.

As seen on theofficequotes.com – Season 5, Episode 18: Blood Drive

> **66**
>
> **Andy:** So, Tuna. When we get in there, let's do a really good job, okay?
> **Jim:** Did that really need to be said?
> **Andy:** Well not everything a guy says needs to be said. Sometimes it—s just about the music of the conversation.
>
> **99**

When your life revolves around acapella, there really is music in everything.

As seen on fanpop.com – Season 3,
Episode 20: Product Recall

"

Andy: Beer me!
Jim: What's that?
Andy: Hand me that water. I always say,
'Beer me.' Gets a laugh like a quarter
of the time.
Jim: Lord, beer me strength. **"**

*Although he doesn't warm to "beer me"
straight away, Jim eventually embraces and
starts to use it.*

As seen on tvfanatic.com – Season 3,
Episode 20: Product Recall

"

When I was in college, I used to get wicked hammered. My nickname was 'Puke'. I would chug a fifth of So-Co, sneak into a frat party, polish off a few people's empties, some brewskies, some Jell-O shots, do some body shots off myself, pass out, wake up the next morning, boot, rally, more So-Co, head to class. Probably would have gotten expelled if I'd let it affect my grades, but I aced all my courses.

Dunder Mifflin

They called me 'Ace'. It was totally awesome. I got straight B's. They called me 'Buzz'.

99

Andy Bernard

The halcyon days of Broccoli Rob and Here Comes Treble at Cornell (ever heard of it?) were always firmly in Andy's rear-view mirror.

As seen on imdb.com – Season 5 Episode 10: Moroccan Christmas

---

66

Women cannot resist a man singing show tunes. It's so powerful, even a lot of men can't resist a man singing show tunes.

99

Andy Bernard

One's phone going off in the middle of singing those show tunes might put them off though.

As seen on kidadl.com, January 26, 2021, by Kidadl Team

66

Andy: You can't let a girl feel good about herself. It will backfire on you. Every compliment has to be backhanded. 'Oh I like your dress, but I'd like it more if you had prettier hair.'

Pam: That's psychotic. Do guys actually do that?

Jim: Well guys with girlfriends don't.

Andy: That's low, Tuna.

99

Andy, Pam and Jim try to help Kevin land the woman of his dreams – with varying degrees of success.

As seen on tvfanatic.com – Season 5, Episode 17: Golden Ticket

66

I wake up every morning in a bed that's too small, drive my daughter to a school that's too expensive, and then I go to work to a job for which I get paid too little. But on pretzel day? Well, I like pretzel day. **99**

Stanley Hudson

No one hates their job more than Stanley, and despite it all there's still a fleeting moment of redemption.

As seen on readbeach.com - Season 3, Episode 5: Initiation

"

If I don't have some cake soon,
I might die.

"

Stanley Hudson

*Everyone wants to think they're Jim or Pam,
but deep down we're all Stanley.*

As seen on goalcast.com, April 27, 2020,
by Flavia Medrut

"

I do not like pregnant women in my workspace. They're always complaining. I have varicose veins, too. I have swollen ankles. I'm constantly hungry. Do you think my nipples don't get sore too? Do you think I don't need to know the fastest way to the hospital? **"**

Stanley Hudson

Stanley raises a solid point.

As seen on readbeach.com – Season 5, Episode 3: Baby Shower

"

I don't wanna be, like, a guy here, you know? Like, Stanley is the crossword-puzzle guy and Angela has cats. I don't wanna have a thing here. You know, I don't wanna be the 'something guy.'

"

Ryan Howard

But Ryan did become a guy. He became "Fire Guy", then "Fired Guy", then "Hired Guy".

As seen on officetally.com – Season 2,
Episode 4: The Fire

"

Last year, Creed asked me how to set up a blog. Wanting to protect the world from being exposed to Creed's brain, I opened up a Word document on his computer and put an address at the top. I've read some of it. Even for the Internet, it's pretty shocking. **"**

Ryan Howard

Thankfully Ryan protected the world from the dark and twisted mind of Creed Bratton.

As seen on grizly.com – Season 3,
Episode 23: The Job

66

Yeah, I'm not a temp anymore. I got Jim's old job, which means at my 10-year high school reunion, it will not say, 'Ryan Howard is a temp.' It will say, 'Ryan Howard is a junior sales associate at a mid-range paper supply firm.' That'll show them.

99

Ryan Howard

Dunder Mifflin Scranton became Ryan's Hotel California – he checked out a few times but he never left.

As seen on tvquot.es – Season 3,
Episode 1: Gay Witch Hunt

66

Ryan: Jim. I wanted to apologize...
for how I treated you last year. I
lost sight of myself and now that
I've quit the rat race I've realized
there's so much more to life than
being the youngest VP in the
company's history. I've even started
volunteering. Giving back to the
community.

Jim: Well that's great. You're talking
about your court-ordered community
service?

Dunder Mifflin

Ryan: I don't need a judge to tell me to keep my community clean.
Jim: But he did, right?

"

Jim and Ryan never really clicked, so why not get a jab in at the guy who made your life hell when he was your superior too?.

As seen on tvfanatic.com – Season 5,
Episode 1: Weight Loss

"

Look, it doesn't take a genius to know that every organization thrives when it has two leaders. Go ahead, name a country that doesn't have two presidents. A boat that sets sail without two captains. Where would Catholicism be without the Popes?

"

Oscar Martinez

Oscar is not impressed with Jim and Michael being co-managers.

As seen on tvfanatic.com – Season 6, Episode 3:
The Promotion

"

Besides having sex with men, I would say the Finer Things Club is the gayest thing about me. **"**

Oscar Martinez

There's no place for the unrefined in Scranton's most exclusive club.

"

You see, I sit across from a man. I see his face. I see his eyes. Now, does it matter if he wants a hundred dollars of paper or a hundred million dollars of deep-sea drilling equipment?

Don't be a fool. He wants respect. He wants love. He wants to be younger. He wants to be attractive. There is no such thing as a product. Don't ever think there is.

There is only... sex.

Everything... is sex. You understand that what I'm telling you is a universal truth... Toby?

99

Robert California

A man so intimidating, persuasive and enigmatic that he convinced the CEO of a company to make him CEO instead.

As seen on michaelscottpod.com – 98: Robert California

66

Dwight: You don't know me! Anything about me! Get out of my head! Stop trying to figure me out. Do you even know anything about paper? How it's made?

Robert: I saw an episode of how they make paper on *Sesame Street*.

Dwight: Get out.

99

Dwight struggles to comprehend that anyone doesn't love and respect paper as much as him.

As seen on officequotes.net – Season 7,
Episode 24: Search Committee

> **66**
>
> Well, I will not be blackmailed by some ineffectual, privileged, effete, soft-penised debutante. You wanna start a street fight with me, bring it on, but you're gonna be surprised by how ugly it gets. You don't even know my real name. I'm the f**king lizard king. **99**

Robert California

a.k.a Bob Kazamakis a.k.a The Lizard King does not take kindly to Andy threatening him.

As seen on tvquot.es – Season 8,
Episode 23: Turf War

That's what they said

"

Women reach their sexual peak at whatever age Jan was last week. I mean it was... like making love with a wild animal. But not like a cougar like you might think. It was, uh, like a swarm of bees. Bees that just find something wrong with every hotel room. **"**

Clark

Clark and Plop were not popular inclusions in the final season, but Clark certainly went the extra mile to land Jan as a client.

As seen on imdb.com – Season 9,
Episode 11: Suit Warehouse

"

Well, I was in the Seminary for a year and dropped out 'cause I wanted to have sex with this girl, Cathy. Followed her to Scranton. Took the first job I could find in HR. Later she divorced me. So no, I wouldn't say I have a passion for HR. **"**

Toby Flenderson
A peek behind the curtain of a sad life.

As seen on tvfanatic.com – Season 5,
Episode 26: Casual Friday

"

Dwight: Hey, Toby… You said that we could come to you if we had any questions.

Toby: Sure.

Dwight: Where is the clitoris? On a website, it said, 'At the crest of the labia.' What does that mean?

What does the female vagina look like?

Dunder Mifflin

Toby: [To camera] Technically, I am in Human Resources, and Dwight was asking about human anatomy.

I'm just sad the public school system failed him so badly. **99**

The first, but not the last, time Dwight has questions about vaginas for Toby.

As seen on imdb.com – Season 2, Episode 2: Sexual Harassment

"

No matter how many times I reach out to Dwight, he doesn't seem to want anything to do with me. It reminds me of my relationship with my son. Except there, I'm the Dwight.

"

Deangelo Vickers

It's hard to believe Deangelo's juggling routine didn't help him connect with his son

As seen on imdb.com – Season 7,
Episode 22: The Inner Circle

❝

Holly is ruining Michael's life. He thinks she is so special. And she's so not. Her personality is like a 3. Her sense of humor is a 2. Her ears are like a 7 and a 4. Add it all up and what do you get? 16. And he treats her like she's a perfect 40. It's nuts.

❞

Erin Hannon

Erin never mentions how Andy and Gabe stack up on her "perfect 40" scale.

As seen on quotecatalog.com – Season 7,
Episode 14: The Search

That's what they said

66

I cannot believe that Andy is throwing a party like this just to impress the CEO. Classic Gabe move. Hey, Andy, how about you don't steal my business strategies, and I won't dress like my life is just one long brunch? **99**

Gabe Lewis

Andy and Gabe clashed many times over Erin and both lost. Many times.

As seen on tvquot.es - Season 8,
Episode 4: Garden Party

66

Gabe: Okay. So, PDAs. That's gonna include behaviors such as hugging, kissing, uh...

Kevin: Booby honking.

Gabe: Yeah, booby honking. Sure.

Kevin: Butt honking.

Gabe: Butt honking. Yeah, all the honking.

99

It's important to be clear about what is and isn't okay in the office – especially when Michael and Holly couldn't keep their hands off each other.

As seen on ew.com – Season 7, Episode 15: PDA

> ❝
>
> I taught Mike some, uh, phrases to help with his interracial conversations. You know, stuff like, 'Fleece it out.' 'Going mach five.' 'Dinkin' flicka.' You know, things us Negroes say. ❞

Darryl Philbin

Darryl had no time for Michael, but still showed up when he needed him. Even if it included "pippity poppity give me the zoppity".

As seen on officequotes.net – Season 2, Episode 22: Casino Night

"

My future isn't going to be determined by seven little white lotto balls. It's going to be determined by two big black balls.

"

Darryl Philbin

And Darryl's big black balls took him all the way from the warehouse to a successful sports marketing job in Austin.

As seen on quotecatalog.com – Season 8, Episode 3: Lotto

"

Kelly: Well, I just need to know where this is going.

Darryl: Hey, I like you. All right? What's not to like? But you need to access your un-crazy side; otherwise, maybe this thing has run its course…

Kelly: Darryl Philbin is the most complicated man that I've ever met. I mean, who says exactly what they're thinking? What kind of game is that?

"

Kelly and Darryl didn't last. She was only with him to make Ryan jealous and he couldn't handle her Kelly-ness.

As seen on theoffice.fandom.com – Dunderpedia: The Office Wiki

66

I'd better come out of this smelling like a rose. I've been on my best behavior for nine years. If it wasn't for the cameras, I would've done some truly vulgar crap. 99

Meredith Palmer

Thank goodness for that, Meredith.

As seen on buzzfeed.com, February 18, 2021, by Ahsoka400

That's what they said

___

“

Who's the one who didn't bring lice into the office? Meredith. Sure I gave everybody pink eye once, and my ex keyed a few of their cars, and yeah I BMed in the shredder on New Year's. But I didn't bring the lice in. That was all Pam.

”

Meredith Palmer

Meredith lived hard but still managed to get her PhD in psychology while tearing it up.

As seen on officetally.com – Season 9,
Episode 10: Lice

___

"

Me mechanic not speak English. But he know what me mean when me say 'car no go', and we best friends.
So me think: why waste time, say lot word when few word do trick?

"

Kevin Malone

Kevin is not a man who could afford for people to think he was more stupid.

As seen on officequotes.net – Season 8, Episode 2: The Incentive

66

Michael: Meredith, why don't you tell
Holly it's not what she thinks, nothing
unethical happened, and that you just
like to sleep around.

Meredith: Am I in trouble here or
something?

Michael: No. No. This is just a stupid
formality.

Holly: No, it's not a formality. Now,
were these meet-ups, just personal,
unrelated to business?

Meredith: Nah. I wouldn't have done it if
it wasn't for the discount paper. There's
not a lot of fruit in those looms.

Dunder Mifflin

Michael: For the love of God, we're trying to help you, you stupid bag.

Holly: What I don't understand is why the steak coupons? I mean, if you were already getting the discounted paper?

Meredith: Well, it's funny. Maybe it's a girl thing, but after we did it, when he would give me those coupons, I just felt good about myself. **99**

Meredith was always willing to go the extra mile to help Dunder Mifflin.

As seen on tigerdroppings.com – Season 5, Episode 2: Business Ethics

---

> **"**
>
> The weird thing is now I'm exactly where I want to be. I've got my dream job at Cornell, and I'm still just thinking about my old pals. Only now they're the ones I made here. I wish there was a way to know you're in 'the good old days', before you've actually left them.
>
> **"**

Andy spent his whole life searching for what he'd already found.

As seen on women.com, April 5, 2020, by Ashley Ferraro